interchange

THIRD EDITION

Jack C. Richards

VIDEO ACTIVITY BOOK

CAMBRIDGE UNIVERSITY PRESS
Cambridge, New York, Melbourne, Madrid, Cape Town, Singapore,
São Paulo, Delhi, Dubai, Tokyo, Mexico City

Cambridge University Press
32 Avenue of the Americas, New York, NY 10013–2473, USA

www.cambridge.org
Information on this title: www.cambridge.org/9780521602136

First published 1996
7th printing 2010

Printed in Hong Kong, China, by Golden Cup Printing Company Limited

A catalog record for this publication is available from the British Library.

ISBN 978-0-521-60213-6 Video Activity Book 2

Art direction, book design, and layout services: Adventure House, NYC

Plan of Video Activity Book 2

Introduction

INTERCHANGE THIRD EDITION

Interchange Third Edition is a revision of *New Interchange,* the world's most successful and popular English course. *Interchange Third Edition* is a multi-level course in English as a second or foreign language for young adults and adults. The course covers the four skills of listening, speaking, reading, and writing, as well as pronunciation and vocabulary. Particular emphasis is placed on listening and speaking. The primary goal of the course is to teach communicative competence, that is, the ability to communicate in English according to the situation, purpose, and roles of the participants. The language used in *Interchange Third Edition* is American English; however, the course reflects the fact that English is the major language of international communication and is not limited to any one country, region, or culture. Level Two is for students at the low-intermediate level.

Level Two builds on the foundations for accurate and fluent communication already established in *Intro* and Level One by extending grammatical, lexical, and functional skills. The syllabus covered in Level Two also incorporates a rapid review of language from Level One, allowing Student's Book 2 to be used with students who have not studied with Level One.

THE VIDEO COURSE

Interchange Third Edition Video 2 can be used with either *Interchange Third Edition* or *New Interchange.* The Video is designed to complement the Student's Book or to be used independently as the basis for a short listening and speaking course.

As a complement to the Student's Book, the Video provides a variety of entertaining and instructive live-action sequences. Each video sequence provides further practice related to the topics, language, and vocabulary introduced in the corresponding unit of the Student's Book.

As the basis for a short, free-standing course, the Video serves as an exciting vehicle for introducing and practicing useful conversational language used in everyday situations.

The Video Activity Book contains a wealth of activities that reinforce and extend the content of the Video, whether it is used to supplement the Student's Book or as the basis for an independent course. The Video Teacher's Guide provides thorough support for both situations.

COURSE LENGTH

The Video contains a mix of entertaining, dramatized sequences and authentic documentaries for a total of sixteen sequences. These vary slightly in length, but in general, the sequences are approximately five to seven minutes each.

The accompanying units in the Video Activity Book are designed for maximum flexibility and provide anywhere from 45 to 90 minutes of classroom activity. Optional activities described in the Video Teacher's Guide may be used to extend the lesson as needed.

COURSE COMPONENTS

Video

The sixteen video sequences complement Units 1 through 16 of Student's Book 2. There are ten dramatized sequences and six documentary sequences. Although linked to the topic of the corresponding Student's Book unit, each dramatized sequence presents a new situation and introduces characters who do not appear in the text. Each documentary sequence is based on authentic, unscripted interviews with people in various situations, and serves to illustrate how language is used by real people in real situations. This element of diversity helps keep students' interest high and also allows the Video to be used effectively as a free-standing course. At the same time, the language used in the video sequences reflects the structures and vocabulary of the Student's Book, which is based on an integrated syllabus that links grammar and communicative functions.

Video Activity Book

The Video Activity Book contains sixteen units that correspond to the video sequences, and is designed to facilitate the effective use of the Video in the classroom. Each unit includes previewing, viewing, and postviewing activities that provide learners with step-by-step support and guidance in understanding and working with the events and language of the sequence. Learners expand their cultural awareness, develop skills and strategies for communicating effectively, and use language creatively.

Video Teacher's Guide

The Video Teacher's Guide contains detailed suggestions for how to use the Video and the Video Activity Book in the classroom, and includes an overview of video teaching techniques, unit-by-unit notes, and a range of optional extension activities. The Video Teacher's Guide also includes answers to the activities in the Video Activity Book and photocopiable transcripts of the video sequences.

■ VIDEO IN THE CLASSROOM

The use of video in the classroom can be an exciting and effective way to teach and learn. As a medium, video both motivates and entertains students. The *Interchange Third Edition* Video is a unique resource that does the following:

- Depicts dynamic, natural contexts for language use.
- Presents authentic language as well as cultural information about speakers of English through engaging story lines.
- Enables learners to use visual information to enhance comprehension.
- Focuses on the important cultural dimension of learning a language by actually showing how speakers of the language live and behave.
- Allows learners to observe the gestures, facial expressions, and other aspects of body language that accompany speech.

■ WHAT THE VIDEO ACTIVITY BOOK CONTAINS

Each unit of the Video Activity Book is divided into four sections: *Preview*, *Watch the Video*, *Follow-up*, and *Language Close-up*. In general, these four sections include, but are not limited to, the following types of activities:

Preview

Culture The culture previews introduce the topics of the video sequences and provide important background and cultural information. They can be presented in class as reading and discussion activities, or students can read and complete them as homework.

Vocabulary The vocabulary activities introduce and practice the essential vocabulary of the video sequences through a variety of interesting tasks.

Guess the Story/Guess the Facts The Guess the Story (or in some units Guess the Facts) activities allow students to make predictions about characters and their actions by watching the video sequences without the sound or by looking at photos in the Video Activity Book. These schema-building activities help to improve students' comprehension when they watch the sequences with the sound.

Watch the Video

Get the Picture These initial viewing activities help students gain global understanding of the sequences by focusing on gist. Activity types vary from unit to unit, but typically involve watching for key information needed to complete a chart, answer questions, or put events in order.

Watch for Details In these activities, students focus on more detailed meaning by watching and listening for specific information to complete tasks about the story line and the characters or the information in the documentaries.

What's Your Opinion? In these activities, students respond to the sequences by making inferences about the characters' actions, feelings, and motivations, and by stating their opinions about issues and topics.

Follow-up

Role Play, Interview, and Other Expansion Activities This section includes communicative activities based on the sequences in which students extend and personalize what they have learned.

Language Close-up

What Did They Say? These cloze activities focus on the specific language in the sequences by having students watch and listen in order to fill in missing words in conversations.

Grammar and Functional Activities In these activities, which are titled to reflect the structural and functional focus of a particular unit, students practice, in a meaningful way, the grammatical structures and functions presented in the video sequences.

1 What do you miss most?

1 CULTURE

The United States is a country of immigrants. Until the 1960s, most immigrants came from Europe. Today, most come from Latin America and Asia, but there are some immigrants from almost every country in the world. In California, one elementary school has students from 23 different countries. In New York State, another school has students who speak 36 different languages. In both schools, lunch includes foods from many countries, and most students have friends from different cultures. Still, students get homesick. "I like it here, but sometimes I miss what I left behind," says Ji Eun Park, a Korean immigrant to New York.

Are there immigrants in your country? Where are they from?
Do you have friends from other countries? Which countries?
What do you think immigrants miss? Name two things.

2 VOCABULARY Immigrant interviews

Pair work Put three more items in each column. (Most can go in both columns.) Then compare around the class.

architecture	friends	nature	sports
✓family gatherings	holidays	professions	traditions
food	music and dance	✓skills	

Things immigrants bring with them	*Things immigrants miss*
skills	family gatherings

3 GUESS THE FACTS

Watch the video with the sound off. What things in Exercise 2 do you think these people miss about their countries? Circle them.

4 GET THE PICTURE

Complete the chart. Fill in each person's country of origin. Then add one
more piece of information. Compare with a partner.

1 First name:
Shiru

Country:
Japan

Other:
Worked in a bank

2 First name:
Carmen

Country:
....

Other:
....

3 First name:
Adan

Country:
....

Other:
....

4 First name:
Rocky

Country:
....

Other:
....

5 First name:
Cecilia

Country:
....

Other:
....

6 First name:
Nancy

Country:
....

Other:
....

5 WATCH FOR DETAILS

Check (✓) **True** or **False**. Then correct the false statements. Compare
with a partner.

	True	False	
1. Shiru's grandfather lived in Chicago.	☐	☑	*Shiru's uncle lived in Chicago.*
2. Shiru has his own business.	☐	☐	....
3. Carmen's aunt sent her to dance classes.	☐	☐	....
4. Carmen doesn't dance now.	☐	☐	....
5. Adan moved to the U.S. in 1992.	☐	☐	....
6. Adan still enjoys soccer.	☐	☐	....
7. Rocky got a scholarship to study in the U.S.	☐	☐	....
8. Rocky became a nurse in South Africa.	☐	☐	....
9. Cecilia enjoyed horseback riding in Sweden.	☐	☐	....
10. Cecilia's husband doesn't miss Europe.	☐	☐	....

6 WHAT DO THEY REMEMBER?

What do these people miss or remember most about their home countries?
Check (✓) all correct answers. Then compare with a partner.

	1 Shiru	**2** Carmen	**3** Adan	**4** Rocky	**5** Cecilia	**6** Nancy
Christmas	☐	☐	☐	☐	☐	☐
evening classes	☐	☐	☐	☐	☐	☐
family	☐	☐	☐	☐	☐	☐
food	☑	☐	☐	☐	☐	☐
making dolls	☐	☐	☐	☐	☐	☐
mountains	☑	☐	☐	☐	☐	☐
people and friends	☑	☐	☐	☐	☐	☐
rivers and hills	☐	☐	☐	☐	☐	☐
the beauty	☐	☐	☐	☐	☐	☐

Follow-up

7 DIFFICULT CHOICES

A *Group work* Add two questions to the list.
Then interview three classmates
and complete the chart.

I'd like to move to Australia.

	Classmate 1	Classmate 2	Classmate 3
1. Would you like to move to a new country? Which one?			
2. What would you miss most?			
3. What would your biggest problem be?			
4.			
5.			

B *Class activity* Compare answers as a class.

Language close-up

8 WHAT DID THEY SAY?

Nancy Kim is interviewing immigrants from different countries.

A Watch the first interview. What questions does Nancy ask Shiru?
Fill in the blanks. Then act out the interview with a partner.

1. Shiru, where ....*are*.... ....*you*.... ....*from*..... originally?
2. Why did .... here?
3. How long .... here in the United States?
4. How old .... you came?
5. Did you .... in Japan?
6. What .... now?
7. What do you .... Japan?

B Now watch the next interview. Write the questions Nancy asks
Carmen. Then act out the interview with a partner.

1. *What's your name?* ....
2. ....
3. ....
4. ....
5. ....
6. ....
7. ....

9 PAST TENSE QUESTIONS *Finding out about someone*

A Complete the questions with the phrases in the box. Then add two
questions of your own.

1. Where ...*were you born*.. ?
2. Did you have .... ?
3. Did you play... ?
4. Where did you .... ?
5. Did you study .... ?
6. Did you work .... ?
7. .... ?
8. .... ?

> a happy childhood
> part-time in high
>   school
> go to high school
> ✓were you born
> English in high school
> any special games as a
>   child

B *Pair work* Interview a classmate. Take turns asking and answering
the questions.

2 Wait for me!

1 *CULTURE*

Vancouver, British Columbia, is a young city – just over 100 years old. When British Columbia became part of Canada in the 1870s, Vancouver wasn't even a town. But when Captain George Vancouver arrived in 1792, he saw Vancouver's natural beauty and talked about it to other explorers. The city is surrounded by water on three sides and mountains to the north. Visitors also enjoy famous sites such as Stanley Park and Chinatown, and they can even see the city from the window of a seaplane.

The seaplane: a great way to see the city!

Would you like to visit Vancouver?
What other interesting facts do you know about Canada?

2 *VOCABULARY* Locations

Pair work Imagine that you are visiting Stanley Park in Vancouver. Ask about the location of places in the park. Use the map and some of these words.

across from	between	near	straight ahead
behind	just past	not far from	to the right/left

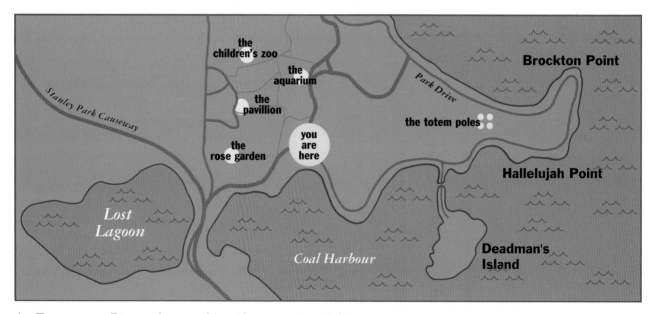

A: Excuse me. Do you know where the aquarium is?
B: It's straight ahead.

3 GUESS THE STORY

Watch the first two minutes of the video with the sound off.
These people are taking a tour of Vancouver. What do you think
the problem is? Check (✓) your answer.

☐ The tourists can't see the things they want to see.
☐ They can't spend enough time at each place.
☐ Someone on the tour is too talkative.
☐ The tour guide doesn't know the answers to questions.
☐ The tour van is uncomfortable.

Watch the video

 GET THE PICTURE

A Look at your answer to Exercise 3. Did you guess correctly?

B Check (✓) the things the tour group did. Then compare
with a partner.

☑ They visited Stanley Park.
☐ They saw a famous collection of totem poles.
☐ They went to the aquarium.
☐ They took a ride on the seaplane.
☐ They drove to Cypress Mountain.
☐ They stopped at a restaurant for lunch.

5 WATCH FOR DETAILS

What did you learn about Vancouver? Check (✓) the correct
answers. Then compare with a partner.

1. Stanley Park is
   ☑ in the center of Vancouver.
   ☐ a few miles from the city center.

2. The totem poles in Stanley Park
   are from
   ☐ British Columbia.
   ☐ France.

3. Cypress Mountain is known for
   ☐ its scenic overlook.
   ☐ its trees.

4. The population of Vancouver is
   ☐ one million.
   ☐ closer to two million.

Wait for me! • **7**

6 WHAT'S YOUR OPINION?

Ted

A *Pair work* Check (✓) the words that describe Ted.
Can you add two words of your own?

annoying	nervous	patient	talkative	....
enthusiastic	outgoing	smart	unfriendly	....

B Do you like tour groups? What are the advantages? The disadvantages?

Follow-up

7 A DAY IN VANCOUVER

A Which of these things would you like to do in Vancouver? Number
them from 1 (most interesting) to 4 (least interesting).

Visit Stanley Park

Take a ride on
the seaplane

Visit Cypress Mountain

Take a walk in
Chinatown

B *Group work* Plan a morning in Vancouver. Choose two things to do.

8 TOURIST INFORMATION

A *Group work* You work for the Tourist Information Center in your city.
Fill in the name of your city. Then complete the chart for visitors.

A BRIEF GUIDE TO .... *(name of city)*	*Our city: some interesting facts* .... *Local foods*	*Buildings and landmarks* .... *Interesting things to do* ....

B Now one student in your group will play the role of Ted. "Ted" will ask lots
of questions about the information in your chart. Try to answer all of them!

9 WHAT DID THEY SAY?

Watch the video and complete the conversation. Then practice it.
Ted is joining a tour group to go sight-seeing in Vancouver.

Ted: Wait for me! Wait, wait for me! Wait for me! Hi.
Good ....*morning*.... . Isn't it a .... day?
Sorry I'm .... , everyone. I couldn't find my
....

Driver: Well, now that we're .... here, we can ....
Our first .... this morning will be Stanley Park.
Stanley Park is .... of the most ....
places in Vancouver . . .

Ted: Sorry. Did you .... Stanley Park? I .... where
Stanley Park .... There must be a .... in here
....

Driver: Stanley Park is .... in the .... of Vancouver.
It's a .... place for .... who live
.... and for ....

Ted: Oh, yes! It .... here that it has a ....
rose .... , a great .... , and a ....
for children.

Driver: Uh, ... As I was .... , . . .

10 INDIRECT QUESTIONS ASKING FOR INFORMATION

A Change these sentences to indirect questions. Begin with **Could you
tell me . . . ?** or **Do you know . . . ?**

1. What time does the tour end? *Could you tell me what time the tour ends?*
2. Where is Stanley Park? ....
3. Where do the totem poles come from? ....
4. What is the population of Vancouver? ....
5. How far are we from the hotel? ....

B *Pair work* Take turns asking and answering the questions using
information from the video.

C *Group work* Now take turns asking indirect questions about other
cities. How many questions can your group answer?

3 A great little apartment

Preview

1 CULTURE

Colleges and universities in the United States and Canada usually provide dormitories for students on campus, but almost 60 percent prefer to live in apartments with friends. In a recent survey, most students said that dormitories have too many rules. Even more said that it was just easier to live with friends. But even friends can have problems when they rent an apartment. The biggest problems: deciding who's going to cook and clean, getting things fixed when they don't work, and living with other people's bad habits.

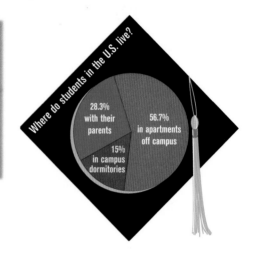

Where do students in the U.S. live?

28.3% with their parents

56.7% in apartments off campus

15% in campus dormitories

Where do university students usually live in your country? Why?
What do you think are some advantages and disadvantages of sharing an apartment with friends?

2 VOCABULARY Apartment hunting

Pair work What do you think are the most important factors in renting an apartment? Number the items below from 1 (most important) to 8 (least important).

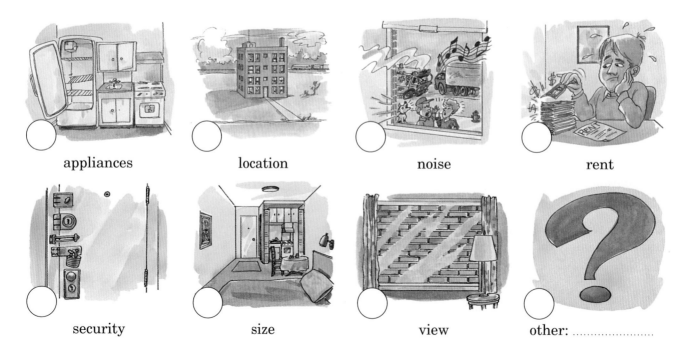

appliances   location   noise   rent

security   size   view   other: ....

Watch the first minute of the video with the sound off.
What don't the young women like about their
apartment? Choose an answer from Exercise 2.

They don't like the ....

Watch the video

4 GET THE PICTURE

How is the current apartment different from the one the young women
look at? Circle the correct answers. Then compare with a partner.

	the current apartment		the apartment they look at	
1. rent	$450	$600	$450	$600
2. location	near school	not near school	near school	not near school
3. size	only 1 room	1 bedroom	2 bedrooms	3 bedrooms

5 WATCH FOR DETAILS

Correct the mistakes below. Then compare with a partner.

Cindy, Karen, and Sue ~~work~~ *are students* at the University of Chicago,
and they want to find a new apartment. They look in the
newspaper. There is a cheaper apartment for rent in
Lakeview. That weekend, they go to see it. The living room
is large, the kitchen is very clean and has a new stove, and
the bedrooms are quiet. Karen and Sue think Cindy should
have her own bedroom. Cindy wants to pay more for it.

Cindy   Karen   Sue

6 A MATTER OF OPINION

A Who holds the opinions below? Check (✓) all correct answers. Then compare with a partner.

	Cindy	Karen	Sue
The current apartment . . .			
is too small.	✓	✓	☐
is in a convenient location.	☐	☐	☐
is in a good neighborhood.	☐	☐	☐
The new apartment . . .			
is expensive.	☐	☐	☐
has a small living room.	☐	☐	☐
has a dirty kitchen.	☐	☐	☐
is too noisy.	☐	☐	☐

B Do you think Cindy, Karen, and Sue will rent the new apartment? If so, should Cindy have her own room? Why or why not?

Follow-up

7 ROLE PLAY Renting an apartment

A *Pair work* Imagine that you want to rent an apartment with two friends. What questions will you need to ask? Make a list.

1. *How much is the rent?*
2. *How many bedrooms does it have?*
3. ....

4. ....
5. ....
6. ....

B *Group work* Now join another pair. Three of you are friends. The fourth person is a rental agent.

Friends: Find out what apartments are available. Then "visit" one of them and ask lots of questions.

Agent: Try to make every apartment you describe sound attractive.

Start like this:

Friend 1: We're looking for an apartment in
          (name of neighborhood) .

  Agent: Well, I've got a great little apartment
          to show you.

Friend 2: *Little?* How big is it? . . .

8 WHAT DID THEY SAY?

Watch the video and complete the conversation. Then practice it.

Cindy thinks she and her roommates should try to find a new apartment.

Cindy: Listen, I know this ......*place*...... is only $450 a ...., but I really
think we .... to find a new ....
It's just not .... enough for the .... of us.

Karen: Well, it is pretty .... , I agree, but the
.... is great. We can ....
to school.

Sue: And I love the ....

Cindy: Yeah, but .... apartment is a .... !

Sue: Well, why don't we .... what's in the .... ?
Maybe we can .... something a little ....

Cindy: Great .... ! . . . Now, let's see what's ....
Oh, here's something .... A two-.....................
apartment in Lakeview for only $................. . That's a great ....

Karen: Yeah, but a .... way from ....

9 EVALUATIONS AND COMPARISONS Giving opinions

A Complete the sentences using **is too** . . . or **isn't . . . enough**, choosing
words from the box. Then compare with a partner. Make sure your sentences
are true in the video! (Some items have more than one answer.)

1. The young women think their apartment ....*is too small*.......... for three people.
2. Karen thinks the new apartment .... to school.
3. Sue thinks $600 .... for rent.
4. Sue thinks the living room ....
5. Karen thinks the stove in the new apartment ....
6. Karen thinks the bedroom .... with the window open.

big
cheap
clean
close
dirty
expensive
quiet
✓ small

B Now compare the two apartments using **as . . . as**. Share your sentences
with a partner.

1. *The new apartment isn't as small as the old one.*
2. ....
3. ....
4. ....
5. ....

C *Pair work* Now compare your own house or apartment to the apartment
the young women look at. Do you think you would like to live there?

4 What's Cooking?

1 CULTURE

Cooking in the United States and Canada is popular with both men and women. There are best-selling cookbooks and popular TV cooking shows to help people learn to cook almost every kind of food. There is even the TV Food Network, which has cooking shows on 24 hours a day. Some of the shows on this network have titles like "Dining Around," "Too Hot Tamales," and "Ready...Set...Cook!" Do people watch? Yes, but most people say they leave the TV on all day on weekends when they clean.

What do you think the programs "Dining Around," "Too Hot Tamales," and "Ready . . . Set . . . Cook!" are about?
Would you like to watch the TV Food Network? Why or why not?
Who likes to cook in your family?

2 VOCABULARY Cooking

Pair work What things can you use to cook chicken? Put the words in the chart. Can you add four more words?

Kitchen appliances	Cooking utensils	Cooking ingredients
a refrigerator	*a frying pan*	*salt*

bread crumbs   butter

flour   ✓ a frying pan

a stove   ✓ salt   ✓ a refrigerator   a saucepan   an oven   oil   a knife

Answer these questions.

1. Who do you think this woman is?

2. What do you think happens?

3. Who do you think this man is?

Watch the video

4 *GET THE PICTURE*

Check (✓) the correct answers. Then compare with a partner.

1. Why is Mark doing the cooking show today?
   - ☐ He has changed jobs.
   - ☐ The chef is sick.
   - ☐ He's learning to cook.

2. What does Mark usually do?
   - ☐ He's a news reporter.
   - ☐ He's a sports reporter.
   - ☐ He's a producer.

3. How successful was Mark as a chef?
   - ☐ Very successful.
   - ☐ OK.
   - ☐ Not very successful.

5 *MAKING INFERENCES*

Which statements are probably true? Which are probably false?
Check (✓) your answers. Then compare with a partner.

	True	False
1. Something Louise ate made her sick.	☐	☐
2. Mark wants to do the cooking show.	☐	☐
3. Mark hasn't cooked Fast Chicken with Oyster Dressing before.	☐	☐
4. The oven is too hot.	☐	☐
5. Mark dries the chicken correctly.	☐	☐
6. Mark uses the right amount of butter.	☐	☐
7. Mark adds too much salt.	☐	☐
8. Mark doesn't know how to close the bird.	☐	☐
9. The producers like Mark's show.	☐	☐
10. Mark will do the show again tomorrow.	☐	☐

6 A SIMPLE MEAL

A *Pair work* Do you know how to make a tuna sandwich? Number the steps (1 to 6). Then practice giving instructions like this:

This is how you make a tuna sandwich:

.... Then put the other slice on top and you have a tuna sandwich.

.... Then open a can of tuna and put the tuna in a bowl.

.... First, take two slices of bread.

.... After that, spread the mixture on one of the slices of bread.

.... Put some lettuce and tomato on top.

.... Then add mayonnaise, salt, pepper, and spices.

B Now write out instructions for your own simple snack, but put the steps in the wrong order. Read the steps out loud. Your partner will put them in the correct order.

A Quick Snack:

------ ---

------ ---

------ ---

------- ---

------ ---

------ ---

7 HOW ABOUT YOU?

Pair work Answer these questions.

1. Do you ever cook at home? Why or why not?
2. What are three dishes that you know how to make?
3. Have you ever had an accident in the kitchen? What happened?

Language close-up

8 WHAT'S THE RECIPE?

Watch the video and complete the recipe. Then compare with a partner.

Here is the recipe Mark Spencer tried to follow.

Fast Chicken with Oyster Dressing

First, turn on the .... to hot.

Next, thoroughly .... the chicken and .... it dry.

Then make the .... stuffing.

In a large .... pan, ... half a cup of ....

Next, cut up a large .... into small .... and put it in the ....

Next, take three .... oysters. .... them up and .... them to the pan.

.... one-half cup of .... caps.

After the .... , add one and a half .... of water. And .... in

three cups of ....

Then add a pinch of ....

Now put the .... in the bird. Then .... the bird.

Now sprinkle .... paprika and add .... to ....

9 SEQUENCE ADVERBS Giving instructions

Put the pictures in order (1 to 8). Then give the *correct* instructions
for each photo, choosing from the verbs in the box. Use the sequence
adverbs **first**, **then**, **next**, **after that**, and **finally**.

add	prepare
cut up	put in
melt	sprinkle
mix in	stir
pat	✓ wash

....
....

....
....

Finally,
....

....
....

1
First, wash the chicken.
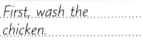

....

....

....

Did anyone see the tent?

Preview

1 *CULTURE*

Every year, millions of people in the United States and Canada go camping. Many bring tents and sleeping bags and go to a park campsite. Some go to quiet wilderness areas with few people. Others go to private campgrounds in vans and trailers. Most people say they camp to get away from everything and everyone. But this is not always possible. At popular parks like Yellowstone National Park and the Grand Canyon, you have to make a reservation for a campsite months in advance – and be prepared for traffic jams!

Have you ever gone camping? Where? When?
What do you think are two enjoyable things and two difficult things about camping?

2 *VOCABULARY* Camping

Pair work What would you take on a camping trip? Put the words in the chart. Can you add three more words?

Camping equipment	Food and drink	Things to enjoy
.a backpack........	....	....
....	....	....
....	....	....
....	....	....
....	....	....

 ✓a backpack   a cassette player   cassette tapes   eggs   fruit

 a guitar   hamburgers   a sleeping bag    a tent   water

3 GUESS THE STORY

A *Watch the first minute of the video with the sound off.*
What things does the family take on the camping trip? Circle
them in Exercise 2.

B Look at the title of the unit. What one important thing can't
the family find? What do you think the reason is?

Watch the video

4 GET THE PICTURE

Check (✓) **True** or **False**. Correct the false statements.
Then compare with a partner.

		True	False	
1.	The boys are looking forward to the trip.	☐	☐	....
2.	The boys leave the sleeping bags at home.	☐	☐	....
3.	The family goes camping anyway.	☐	☐	....

5 WATCH FOR DETAILS

Check (✓) the correct answers. Then compare with a partner.

1. The family hasn't gone camping
   ☐ in a year.
   ☑ in years.

2. The trip to the campsite takes
   ☐ four hours.
   ☐ ten hours.

3. The boys aren't too excited because
   ☐ they're going to miss the baseball game on TV.
   ☐ they don't like insects.

4. Ken took the green bag out of the car
   ☐ to make room for his things.
   ☐ to annoy his parents.

5. On the trip, the boys plan to
   ☐ go fishing and climbing.
   ☐ rest.

6. When they find out they're going to stay in a motel,
   the boys are
   ☐ pleased.
   ☐ disappointed.

GOING CAMPING

A *Group work* Plan a weekend camping trip. First, choose one of the places below or another place that you know.

Now agree on answers to these questions.

1. When are we going to go?
2. How are we going to get there?
3. What are we going to take?
4. How long are we going to stay?
5. What are we going to do each day?

B *Class activity* Compare your plans around the class. Which group planned the most interesting trip?

A GOOD SOLUTION

A *Pair work* Imagine that you are in the same situation as the family, but there is no hotel nearby. What would you do? List at least four more possibilities.

I'd probably . . .

go home.
....
....
....
....

B *Group work* Now take turns making suggestions. Give as many suggestions as you can in two minutes. Who has the most suggestions?

A: We'd better go home.
B: We ought to . . .

Language close-up

8 WHAT DID THEY SAY?

Watch the video and complete the conversations. Then practice them.

Debbie and John are getting ready to go camping with their children.

John: Is all the ....*food*.... ready to ..*go*.. ?

Debbie: Well, I've packed the .... , the rolls, and the
.... Do we need .... else?

John: Oh, we'd .... bring something for
.... What about some .... ?

Debbie: Oh, ...

John: Oh, and .... about .... ? We ....
to bring lots of .... for the ....

Debbie: Good idea. Have you .... all the
.... gear?

John: Yeah, it's all .... the .... , the
.... bags. Uh-huh. Hey, ... is going to
be so much ....

Debbie: Oh, yes. We haven't .... camping in ....

Ken: So what .... we take?

Henry: I'm .... to take my ....

Ken: Great. And I'm going to take my ....

 9 MODALS FOR SUGGESTION

A What suggestions did Debbie and John make? Match the phrases from
columns A and B and write five more sentences. Then compare with a partner.

A   *B*

We'd better   forget anything.
We'd better not   bring something for breakfast.
We should   pack the camping gear.
We shouldn't   leave late if we want to get a good campsite.
We ought to   take traveler's checks and credit cards.
                              bring lots of fruit for the boys.

We'd better bring
something for
breakfast.

1. *We'd better bring something for breakfast.*
2. ....
3. ....
4. ....
5. ....
6. ....

B *Pair work* Imagine that you are about to leave on a camping trip. Give
five more suggestions of your own, using the expressions in Column A above.

6 Oh, I'm sorry!

Preview

1 CULTURE

Over 2 million people in the United States have minor accidents at the office each year. Some of the most common accidents involve slippery floors, pens and pencils, computers, clothing, and carelessness by other workers. Careless people cause thousands of injuries and "headaches" at the workplace every year. Accidents cost employers a lot of money in medical expenses, insurance, and time away from work.

What equipment in an office can be dangerous? What can happen? Do you know any careless people? What do they do?

2 VOCABULARY Requests

A *Pair work* What are they saying? Write one request below each picture.

Can you talk a little more quietly?
✓ Would you mind closing the door?
Could you help me for a minute?

Could you come back a little later?
Please be careful!
Would you get to work right away, please?

Would you mind closing the door?

....

....

....

....

....

B Now make the requests. Have conversations like these:

A: Would you mind closing the door?
B: Sure. No problem.

A: Please be careful!
B: Oh, I'm sorry!

22

3 GUESS THE FACTS

Mike

Watch the first two minutes of the video with the sound off.
Answer these questions.

1. How many things does Mike do that make Jim angry?
2. What do you think Jim says to him?

Jim

Watch the video

4 GET THE PICTURE

A Mike and Elaine are both a little clumsy. What do they do? Fill in
the blanks. Then compare with a partner.

1. Mike knocks over Jim's ...*wastebasket*.... .
2. Mike unplugs Jim's ....

3. Elaine spills .... on the floor.
4. Mike and Elaine bump into each other and
   hit their ....

B Watch again. What other clumsy things do Mike and Elaine do?
Complete the sentences. Then compare with a partner.

1. Mike knocks a mailbox off the ....
2. Mike opens the door and blows papers off
   Jim's ....

3. Elaine drinks hot .... and burns
   her tongue.
4. Elaine shakes Mike's hand with a cup of
   .... in hers.

5 WATCH FOR DETAILS

Correct the mistakes below. Then compare with a partner.

           accidents
Mike is doing a survey on ~~computers~~ in the workplace. Jim is busy,
but he tells Mike to come back at 4:00. Then Mike sees Elaine in
the cafeteria. He wants to know her name. Soon Mike and Elaine
discover that they have a lot in common. They have the same boss.

6 WHAT'S YOUR OPINION?

A *Pair work* Complete the chart. Check (✓) the words that describe how you think Jim, Mike, and Elaine feel.

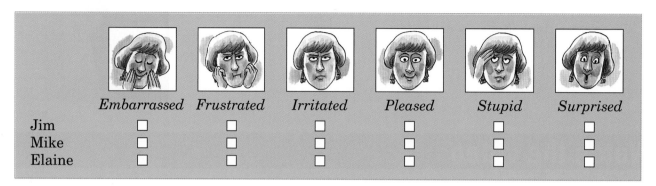

	Embarrassed	Frustrated	Irritated	Pleased	Stupid	Surprised
Jim	☐	☐	☐	☐	☐	☐
Mike	☐	☐	☐	☐	☐	☐
Elaine	☐	☐	☐	☐	☐	☐

B Do you sometimes get irritated with people like Mike and Elaine? What kinds of things irritate you? Give opinions like this:

A: I get irritated when people talk too much.
B: It bothers me when people . . .

Follow-up

7 ROLE PLAY *The next week*

A *Pair work* Imagine that Mike and Elaine met for dinner a week later. What clumsy things did they do? Complete the chart.

Elaine probably . . .

....

....

....

Mike probably . . .

stepped on Elaine's foot. ....

....

....

B Now act out Mike and Elaine's conversation. Start like this:

Mike: Hi, Elaine. How are you? Oh, I'm sorry! Did I step on your foot?
Elaine: It's OK. . . . Whoops! . . .

8 WHAT DID THEY SAY?

Watch the video and complete the conversation. Then practice it.

Jim is working at his desk when Mike approaches him with a request.

Jim: Would you mind ....*closing*.... the ......*door*...... , Mike?

Mike: Huh? Oh, ... , Jim. I'm sorry. Did I .... that?

Jim: It's all ....

Mike: Well, here. Let me .... these .... for you.

Jim: Don't .... I'll get them ....

Mike: I'm .... I didn't see the

....

Jim: It's .... , Mike. I'll take .... of it.

Mike: No, no, no. .... me.

Jim: Please be .... ! My .... is

plugged into the . . . Never ....

Mike: I .... you weren't .... on anything ....

Jim: What is .... that you .... ?

Mike: I'm .... a survey on .... in the ....

Would you like to .... a few .... ?

Jim: Look, I'm awfully .... right now, Mike. Could you ....

back a little .... ?

9 TWO-PART VERBS Making requests

A Match each office item below with at least two of the verbs in the box. Then add three things from your classroom. Which of these verbs do they go with?

1. those papers ....*pick up those papers* .... *put away those papers* ....

2. the fax machine ....

3. the computer ....

4. the report ....

5. the sales figures ....

6. ....

7. ....

8. ....

> pick up
> plug in
> put away
> take out
> turn on
> write down

B *Pair work* Now have conversations like these. First, use the office items. Then practice the conversations again using things from your classroom.

A: Would you mind picking up those papers?
B: Oh, I'm sorry! Did I do that?

A: Could you put away those papers?
B: Sure. No problem.

Great inventions

Preview

CULTURE

Americans and Canadians invent thousands of new gadgets each year, but only a few of them become popular. What kinds of things do people invent? Here are a few ideas that inventors have come up with recently:

- a chair that fits in your pocket
- a pop-up hot dog cooker
- lipstick you can eat
- makeup for pets

Do you think these inventions will be popular? Why or why not? What gadgets are popular in your country?

You can enjoy a hot dog in minutes.

2 VOCABULARY Gadgets and inventions

Pair work Match the words in the box with their definitions below. Then write the correct word under each picture.

ant	✓inventors' congress
exhibitor	shaver
gadget	steering

inventors' congress...... a large meeting where people show new products that they have made

.... the part of a vehicle that the driver turns to make it go in a certain direction

.... a small machine or device that does a useful job

.... a person who shows his or her work to the public

.... an electric razor for removing hair

.... a small insect

1. ....

2. *inventors' congress*...............

3. ....

4. ....

5. ....

6. ....

26

GUESS THE FACTS

What do you think the inventions below are? Write the correct answers on the lines.

a dish for pet food ✓	an underwater pen	an insect house
a machine to make pet food	a shaver	an insect trap

1. _a dish for pet food_

2. ....

3. ....

a beach bike	an orange and milk drink
a golf buggy	an orange and lemon drink

4. ....

5. ....

Watch the video

4 GET THE PICTURE

A Look at your answers to Exercise 3. Did you guess correctly? Correct your answers. Then compare with a partner.

B Now match the people with their inventions. Write the numbers in the boxes.

5 ⑤ WATCH FOR DETAILS

A Check (✓) the correct answers. Then compare with a partner.

1. It doesn't use water.	☐	☐	☐	☐	☑
2. It's good exercise.	☐	☐	☐	☐	☐
3. You can carry it in your pocket when you're not using it.	☐	☐	☐	☐	☐
4. You use it when you go away from home.	☐	☐	☐	☐	☐
5. You can see it in the dark.	☐	☐	☐	☐	☐

B Watch again. Write one more thing about each item.

1. The pet dish: ....
2. The shaver: ....
3. The insect trap: ....
4. The golf buggy: ....
5. The orange and milk drink: ....

6 ⑥ HOW DOES IT WORK?

Pair work Take turns asking about and describing the inventions above. Have conversations like this:

A: What's this?
B: It's called Chow Baby. It's used to . . .

Follow-up

7 ⑦ YOU'RE AN INVENTOR!

Pair work What would you like to invent and why? Complete the chart.
Then share your inventions with your classmates. Who has the best ones?

Things to make housework easier	*Things for leisure activities*
A robot: It can do the cooking.	

Language close-up

8 WHAT DID THEY SAY?

Watch the video and complete the conversations. Then practice them.

The reporter is talking to the inventors of Chow Baby and the shaver.

Yolanda: This looks ....*interesting*.... . Can you .... me how this .... ?

Exhibitor 1: This is Chow .... It's .... to feed your ....
when you're .... from home. You ....
set the .... , the amount of .... , and it
does .... automatically.

Yolanda: It looks .... Thank you very ....

Exhibitor 1: Thank you.

Yolanda: What is this .... ? Is this a .... ?

Exhibitor 2: No. This is a .... You open it up, ...
it around. You .... the button, and the ....
comes out. You .... it on your .... , shave.
Once you're .... , close it, ... it back
in, and .... it back in your ....

Yolanda: .... on the go.

Exhibitor 2: Shaving on the ....

Yolanda: What a great .... !

9 GERUNDS Describing something

A What is each invention used for? Complete each sentence with **used for**
and one of the verbs in the box. Then compare with a partner.

drive
✓ feed
keep
make
shave

1. Chow Baby is ....*used*.... ....*for*.... ....*feeding*.... your pet while you are away.
2. The shaver is .... when you are traveling.
3. The insect trap is .... insects out of your pet's food.
4. The golf buggy is .... yourself around the golf course.
5. The juice machine is .... delicious drinks from milk
and orange concentrate.

B *Pair work* Now describe the things below. Your partner will guess the gadgets.

a bathroom   a microwave   a pair of   a stapler   a thermometer   a vacuum
scale   oven   scissors   cleaner

A: This is used for finding out your weight.
B: Is it a bathroom scale?
A: That's right.

8 Thanksgiving

Preview

1 CULTURE

On the fourth Thursday in November, people in the United States celebrate Thanksgiving. They get together with family and friends, share a special meal, and "give thanks" for what they have. The tradition goes back to 1620, when the first group of Europeans, called Pilgrims, settled in North America. The Pilgrims didn't know how to grow crops in the New World, so the Native Americans helped them. Later, they celebrated the good harvest with a special meal. Today on Thanksgiving Day, families and friends do the very same thing.

How did the tradition of Thanksgiving begin?
Is there a similar holiday in your country? What is it?

In Canada, Thanksgiving is celebrated on the second Monday in October.

2 VOCABULARY Thanksgiving foods

A *Pair work* Put the words in the chart. Check (✓) the ones you think are special Thanksgiving foods.

Main dishes	Side dishes	Dessert
	corn	

corn

cranberry sauce

green beans

B *Watch the first two minutes of the video with the sound off.* How many of these foods do you see? Circle them.

roast turkey with stuffing

pumpkin pie

potato salad

mashed potatoes with gravy

ham

GUESS THE FACTS

What do you think are the most popular Thanksgiving foods?
What do you think people do after the Thanksgiving meal?

Watch the video

 4

GET THE PICTURE

Write two new things you learned about Thanksgiving.
Then compare with a partner.

> NOTES
>
> 1. ....
> 2. ....

5

WATCH FOR DETAILS

What do these people eat on Thanksgiving? Check (✓) all correct
answers. Then compare with a partner.

	1	2	3	4
corn	☐	☐	☐	☐
dirty rice	☐	☐	☐	☐
green beans	☐	☐	☐	☐
greens	☐	☐	☐	☐
mashed potatoes	☐	☐	☐	☐
potato salad	☐	☐	☐	☐
pumpkin pie	☐	☐	☐	☐
sopa	☐	☐	☐	☐
turkey	☐	☐	☐	☐

6

UNTRADITIONAL FOODS

Complete the sentences. Then compare with a partner.

1. Sopa is .... in a .... and garlic sauce. It has
   carrots, ... , corn, and sometimes .... in it.
2. Greens is a tradition from the ....
3. Dirty rice is .... mixed with rice.

greens

7 AFTER DINNER

Frank   *Mark*

What do Frank and Mark have in common? Check (✓) **True** or **False**.
Correct the false sentences. Then compare with a partner.

	True	False	
1. Frank and Mark both like to watch baseball on TV.	☐	☐	....
2. They both have dessert right after the meal.	☐	☐	....
3. Men and women both help with the dishes after dinner.	☐	☐	....

8 WHAT DOES THANKSGIVING MEAN TO THEM?

What did these people say about Thanksgiving? Complete the sentences.
Then compare with a partner.

It's time to ....
....
....

It's a day to ....
.... ,
to give thanks for ....
....
....

I think it means to me that
....
....
....

Follow-up

9 SPECIAL HOLIDAYS

Class activity What is your favorite holiday? Complete the chart. Then
compare answers as a class. How many holidays did your class list?

Name of holiday: ....
1. When is it?
2. What special foods do you eat?
3. What else do you do?
4. What does the holiday mean to you?

Language close-up

10 WHAT DID HE SAY?

Watch the video and complete the description. Then compare with a partner.

Polani Pozzani is explaining the history of Thanksgiving in the United States.

Hi. My .....*name*..... is Polani Pozzani. It's the fourth ....
in November, ... Day in the United States.
Many .... celebrate this ....
with family .... such as this .... Let's take
a .... and see where this .... came from.

In the year .... , some Europeans came to ....
America and .... in what is now
.... They were called the
.... The Pilgrims didn't know how to grow
.... in the New .... , so the ....
Americans helped them. They taught the ....
how to .... corn and squash, or .... ,
how to gather .... , and how to hunt wild
.... The .... and the Native
.... "gave .... " by celebrating the
good .... together.

We still .... the same .... on Thanksgiving – roast ....
with stuffing, cranberry .... , and for dessert, ... pie.

11 RELATIVE CLAUSES OF TIME Describing an event

A Rewrite these sentences with relative clauses of time. Begin with
Thanksgiving is a time when . . . . Then compare with a partner.

1. Melissa invites her relatives over for dinner.
   Thanksgiving is a time when Melissa invites her relatives over for dinner.
2. Frank and Karen eat turkey.
   ....
3. Melissa's grandmother prepares a special Mexican dish called sopa.
   ....
4. Rosalind prepares a Louisiana dish called dirty rice.
   ....
5. Karen gives thanks for the things that have happened during the year.
   ....

B *Pair work* Take turns making statements about special days in your country,
like this:

"New Year's Eve is a time when people dance in the streets."

 # A short history of transportation

Preview

 ## 1 CULTURE

Today . . .

Changes in transportation have come from many different countries. These are some important dates:

1804 The steam locomotive was invented in England.
1863 London's first subway opened.
1881 Electric streetcars appeared in Berlin.
1908 Henry Ford's famous car, the "Model T," took to the road in the United States.
1919 Daily airplane flights began on three routes in Europe.
1964 Japanese high-speed passenger trains began operation between Tokyo and Osaka.

The United States has more railroad tracks than any other country in the world, but most people do not travel by train. Ninety percent of American homes have at least one car, and 88 percent of U.S. workers drive to the office!

How did people travel in your country 100 years ago? 50 years ago? 25 years ago?
How do most people in your country get to work or school?
Do most people own a car?

2 VOCABULARY *Transportation and technology*

A *Pair work* Do you know all of these words? Circle the word in each item that doesn't belong.

1. plane   airport   (van)   jumbo jet

2. skyscraper   automobile   freeway   traffic

3. machine   invention   engine   highway

4. speed   time   problem   distance

5. computer   wheel   fax machine   telephone

B Now choose two words from each item and use them in a sentence, like this:

"There is a large airport with many jumbo jets near my home."

3 GUESS THE FACTS

Look at the pictures. Check (✓) at least two forms of transportation that you think used to be popular. Circle at least two that you think are popular now.

an airplane

a bicycle

a boat

a car

a chariot

an electric train

a helicopter

a rocket

a steam-powered train

a truck

Watch the video

4 GET THE PICTURE

A How has transportation changed? Check (✓) the most popular ways to travel, according to the video. Then compare with a partner.

	1900	1990
1. by steam-powered train	☐	☐
2. by high-speed train	☐	☐
3. by automobile	☐	☐
4. by airplane	☐	☐

B What type of transportation does not exist yet in the United States?

5 WATCH FOR DETAILS

Fill in the blanks. Then compare with a partner.

1. Machines that could go faster than horses were invented around ....100............ years ago.
2. In the first half of the 20th century, most people traveled long distances by ....
3. By 1990, there were more than .... million cars in the United States and Canada.
4. High-speed trains are popular today in countries like .... , ... , and ....
5. In the future, super jumbo jets may carry as many as .... people.

6 WHAT DO THE EXPERTS THINK?

What will transportation be like in the future? Write one idea for each person. Then compare with a partner.

Frank Snowden

....
....

Ellen Brown

....
....

Larry Menzel

....
....

7 WHAT'S YOUR OPINION?

Pair work Answer these questions.

1. Do you agree with the experts' predictions? Which ones?
2. What do you think transportation will be like in the future?

Follow-up

8 YOUR CITY

A *Pair work* In your city or town, what are the advantages and disadvantages of these forms of transportation? Complete the chart. Then compare around the class.

	Advantages	*Disadvantages*
car		
bus		
train		
bicycle		

B Convince another pair to leave their cars at home. Give as many reasons as you can why another form of transportation is better.

Language close-up

9 WHAT DID HE SAY?

Watch the video and complete the reporter's introduction. Then compare with a partner.

Mike Sullivan is talking about the history of transportation in North America.

........*Getting*........ from one ......*city*...... to another means .... a plane, a .... , train, or for many people, ... a car. .... in the United States love their .... – even if they have to .... up with .... like this.

.... families have .... or more cars. The .... of the United States is in .... a history of .... in transportation: first, the building of .... across the .... ; then, the .... of giant .... ; and finally, the development of other .... of transportation such as ....

I'm Mike Sullivan, and .... we're going to .... at some of these forms of .... and how they've .... in the last .... hundred ....

10 TALKING ABOUT THE PAST, PRESENT, AND FUTURE

A Complete each sentence with at least two of the phrases in the box. Then compare with a partner.

In the past, people used to . . .

1. ....

2. ....

Today, many people . . .

3. ....

4. ....

In the future, people will . . .

5. ....

6. ....

> drive a car to work
> travel more by train than
>   they do now
> work more from their homes
> travel by high-speed train in
>   Europe
> travel by high-speed train in
>   the United States
> travel by steam-powered
>   train
> own two or more cars
> travel in super jumbo jets
>   with more than 800 people

B Write two more sentences of your own about transportation in the past, present, and future. Take turns reading them to a partner.

1. ....

2. ....

10 Mistaken identity

Preview

1 CULTURE

Nearly 40 percent of U.S. teenagers have a part-time job. Most of them got work in a fast-food restaurant after they saw an advertisement in the newspaper. One of every 11 people in the U.S. gets his or her first part-time job in a fast-food restaurant. In fact, almost 25 percent of adults have worked in a fast-food restaurant at some time in their lives. Although 62 percent of fast-food workers say they enjoy the job, they don't stay long. The average length of employment is only three months.

What part-time jobs are popular with students in your country? Have you ever had a part-time job? What did you have to do?

Looking for your first job? Try tossing pizzas.

2 VOCABULARY Getting a job

Pair work What questions would a job interviewer ask at a fast-food restaurant? Match the parts of the sentences. Then add two questions of your own.

1. Where did you — want to work here?
2. What are your — find out about this job?
3. Why do you well with children?
4. Do you like qualifications?
5. Do you get along good with money?
6. Are you working with people?
7. ....
8. ....

3 GUESS THE STORY

Watch the first two minutes of the video with the sound on. What do you think happens? Check (✓) your answer.

☐ The receptionist mixes up the applications.
☐ Martha and Bob both interview clowns.
☐ Martha and Bob both interview managers.
☐ The receptionist forgets to schedule the interviews.

Bob Anderson

Martha Bennett

GET THE PICTURE

Complete the sentences. Then compare with a partner.

David

Greg

1. Martha wants to hire a ....
2. Bob wants to hire a ....
3. David Jones applied for the job of ....
4. Greg Jones applied for the job of ....
5. Bob interviewed .... by mistake.
6. Martha interviewed .... by mistake.

 WATCH FOR DETAILS

A Complete the sentences with the correct names. Then put the pictures in order (1 to 6).

✓ Jenny calls ....*David Jones*........ to schedule an interview.

Jenny sends .... to Mr. Anderson.

Jenny sends .... to Ms. Bennett.

.... demonstrates a useful "management technique."

.... juggles for Mr. Anderson.

.... tells .... that they have made a mistake.

B Now write the correct sentence under each picture. Compare with a partner.

Jenny calls David Jones to schedule an interview.

6) WHO SAID WHAT?

Who said the sentences below? Check (✓) the correct answers. Then compare with a partner.

	Martha	Bob	David	Greg
1. Will you see if he can come in . . . tomorrow morning . . . oh, around 10:15?	✓	☐	☐	☐
2. I'd really like to have someone by Saturday.	☐	☐	☐	☐
3. I think I'm good with people.	☐	☐	☐	☐
4. I'm very patient.	☐	☐	☐	☐
5. I worked on weekends while I was in school.	☐	☐	☐	☐
6. We need someone who's very good with money.	☐	☐	☐	☐
7. We're really looking for someone who can make people laugh.	☐	☐	☐	☐
8. How did you know I could use these?	☐	☐	☐	☐

Follow-up

7) INTERVIEW

Pair work Interview a classmate to be the clown or the manager. Use the questions in Exercise 2. Start like this:

A: Where did you find out about this job?
B: Well, I saw your advertisement in the newspaper. . . .

8) JOB SKILLS

A *Pair work* What do a manager and a clown need to be good at? Choose from these phrases and add other ideas of your own.

managing money   working with children
making people laugh   solving problems
getting along with people

A manager needs to be good at managing money. . . .

B *Group work* Now play a game. What do people who do the jobs below need to be good at? Take turns giving your ideas. Think of as many things as you can. The person with the most ideas wins.

a chef   a firefighter   a teacher

C What are you good at? Tell your group. Your classmates will suggest an appropriate career for you!

9 WHAT DID THEY SAY?

Watch the video and complete the conversation. Then practice it.

Martha Bennett and Bob Anderson are arranging some job interviews with their receptionist, Jenny.

Jenny: McDouglas Hamburgers. .....*May*..... I help you? No,
he .... in .... now.
.... I'll .... him
the ....

Martha: Well, I .... one more .... to see
for the .... job.

Jenny: OK. What's his .... ?

Martha: .... Jones. This is his .... Will you
.... if he .... come in for an .... tomorrow
.... oh, around .... ?

Jenny: .... Sure. I'll take .... of it.

Martha: Well, ... you, Jenny.

Bob: Oh, Martha. .... you go, there's .... I need
to .... to you ....

Martha: .... is it, Bob?

Bob: I .... we need to hire a ....

Martha: You know, ... do I. All the other .... have one.

10 SHORT RESPONSES Giving personal information

A Write personal responses to these statements, choosing from the expressions below. Then compare with a partner.

So am I.	Neither am I.	I am.	I'm not.
So do I.	Neither do I.	I do.	I don't.
So can I.	Neither can I.	I can.	I can't.

1. I like working with children. ....
2. I enjoy making people laugh. ....
3. I'm not good at managing money. ....
4. I don't like doing office work. ....
5. I can type reasonably fast. ....
6. I can't speak Italian. ....

I can juggle. *So can I.*

B Now write four new statements about yourself and read them to your partner. Your partner will respond with one of the expressions above.

1. ....   3. ....

2. ....   4. ....

11 On the Santa Fe Trail

Preview

1 CULTURE

Santa Fe, New Mexico, is the second oldest city in the United States. The Spanish founded Santa Fe in 1610, but Native Americans lived in the area for more than 2,000 years before that. Today, the city still shows the influence of both cultures in its unusual architecture, interesting handicrafts, and traditional foods. Hundreds of thousands of tourists visit Santa Fe each year to enjoy its unique Southwest culture, rich history, and beautiful shops, museums, and restaurants.

What do you enjoy doing most when you visit a new city?
Would you like to visit Santa Fe? Why or why not?

2 VOCABULARY Sight-seeing

A *Pair work* What can you do when you visit an old, historic town? Put the words in the chart. Can you add two more words?

✓churches   historic places   monuments   palaces   souvenirs
  handicrafts   jewelry   museums   pottery

Places to see and visit		Things to buy	
churches			

B Which things in your chart do you like to do the most?

3 GUESS THE STORY

Watch the first minute of the video with the sound off.
Answer these questions.

Do these people know each other well?
Who do you think lives in Santa Fe?

Pat   Lynne   Bill

42

GET THE PICTURE

A These are the things Pat, Bill, and Lynne did in Santa Fe. Put the pictures in order (1 to 5).

B Now write the correct sentence under each picture. Compare with a partner.

They visited the museum in the Palace of the Governors.
They tried some southwestern food.

They looked at the handicrafts.
They drove down the Santa Fe Trail.
✓ They walked through the Central Plaza.

....
....

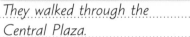
They walked through the Central Plaza.

....
....

....
....

....
....

5 **WHAT'S YOUR OPINION?**

A *Pair work* Is Bill a good tourist? Did he want to do any of the things in Exercise 4? Write **Bill** next to them.

B Now complete the chart about the three people. Check (✓) the words that describe Bill, Lynne, and Pat. Add one word of your own.

	Easygoing	Enthusiastic	Fun to be with	Hard to please	Helpful	....
Bill	☐	☐	☐	☐	☐	☐
Lynne	☐	☐	☐	☐	☐	☐
Pat	☐	☐	☐	☐	☐	☐

6 WATCH FOR DETAILS

Write one thing that you learned about the people, places, or things below. Then compare with a partner.

1. The Native Americans and the Spanish ....
2. The Central Plaza ....
3. The Palace of the Governors ....
4. The Santa Fe Trail ....
5. Some houses in Santa Fe ....
6. Southwestern food ....

Follow-up

7 A DAY IN SANTA FE

Group work Use your knowledge of Santa Fe to plan three things to do. Choose from the suggestions in the tourist brochure below.

Santa Fe

Enjoy the Central Plaza.

Visit the Palace of the Governors.

Come see the beautiful handicrafts.

Take a ride down the Santa Fe Trail.

Stop at the San Miguel Mission.

Try some distinctive southwestern food.

Start like this:

A: Let's go to the Central Plaza, the oldest part of the city.
B: The oldest part of the city? When was it built? . . .

Language close-up

 ## 8 WHAT DID THEY SAY?

Watch the video and complete the conversation. Then practice it.

Lynne and Bill are waiting for their friend Pat to take them sight-seeing in Santa Fe.

Lynne: Oh, here .....*comes*..... Pat.

Pat: Hi, ...

Lynne: What perfect .... !

Pat: Hey, it's .... to see you.

Bill: .... to see you, ...

Lynne: You know, Pat, we couldn't .... We started to
.... the trip the .... you .... here.

Pat: I'm so .... you guys could come for a ....
I can't .... to show you .... Are you
.... ?

Bill: Sure. I've got my .... right here.

Lynne: .... , too.

Pat: Well, ... are we .... for? .... on. . . .
We might as .... start at the Central Plaza, the ....
part of the ....

Lynne: What a .... place!

Pat: Yeah, it's one of my .... It was ....
by the Spanish .... after they arrived in ....

Bill: Wow! The Spanish .... here a .... time.

9 THE PASSIVE Giving factual information

A Imagine that Pat said these things about Santa Fe. Complete the
sentences using the verbs in parentheses. Then compare with a partner.

1. The Central Plaza ...*is*... ......*used*...... as a market.   (use)
2. Spanish .... still .... around here.   (speak)
3. Lots of handicrafts .... in front of the
   museum.   (sell)
4. Adobe houses .... of mud.   (make)
5. Local stones .... to make jewelry.   (use)
6. Southwestern food .... here.   (serve)

B Now write five sentences about your own city using the passive.
Compare around the class.

1. ....
2. ....
3. ....
4. ....
5. ....

Welcome back to West High!

1 *CULTURE*

Each summer, almost every high school in the United States and Canada has class reunions. At these parties, high school classmates get together after many years to relive memories and catch up on news. The most popular reunions are after 10, 20, and 25 years. According to a recent survey, the most common reasons for going to high school reunions include: to see how people have changed, to see old boyfriends and girlfriends, and to talk about recent accomplishments.

A high school reunion is a good time to catch up with old friends.

Are high school reunions common in your country?
Would you like to go to a 10-year class reunion at your high school? Why or why not?
How do you think you will change in the next ten years?

2 *VOCABULARY*

Pair work Put the words in the word map. Can you add four more words?

✓baseball	drama	examinations	graduation	reunion
classmate	English	geometry	librarian	teacher

Subjects		People
....		....
....		....
....		....
....		....

HIGH SCHOOL

Special events		After-school activities
....		*baseball* ....
....		....
....		....
....		....

GUESS THE STORY

A Look at these graduation photos. What do you think these people were like in high school? Write at least one answer for each person.

good at sports
interested in cooking
outgoing and popular
quiet and serious

B Now look at some recent photos. What do you think these people do now? Match.

unemployed at the moment
well-known novelist
is trying to get into the travel business
owns a restaurant
not sure, but doesn't look successful

Jenny

....
....
....

Jenny

....
....
....

Ted

....
....
....

Ted

....
....
....

Don

....
....
....

Don

....
....
....

Kate

....
....
....

Kate

....
....
....

Marie

....
....
....

Marie

....
....
....

Watch the video

4
GET THE PICTURE

Look at your answers to Exercise 3. Did you guess correctly? Correct your answers. Then compare with a partner.

5 WATCH FOR DETAILS

Check (✓) **True** or **False**. Then correct the false statements. Compare with a partner.

	True	False	
1. In high school, Ted planned to be an actor.	☐	☐	....
2. Kate, Marie, and Don were in the same Spanish class.	☐	☐	....
3. Don's novel isn't selling well.	☐	☐	....
4. Don's wife is a television reporter.	☐	☐	....
5. Jenny went to cooking school after she graduated from college.	☐	☐	....
6. Kate and Marie have very good jobs.	☐	☐	....

6 WHAT'S YOUR OPINION?

A *Pair work* Which words are positive? Which are negative? Write **P** or **N** next to each one. (If you don't know the meaning of a word, check your dictionary.)

..*P*.. good-natured .... intelligent .... self-confident .... successful

.... insecure .... modest .... sophisticated .... superficial

B Which words describe these people now? Put at least two words in each column. Can you add one word of your own?

Kate and Marie	Don	Jenny
....	....	....
....	....	....
....	....	....
....	....	....

Follow-up

7 ROLE PLAY Class Reunion

Group work Imagine that you go to a class reunion in 10 years. Now you are very successful. Greet your former classmates. Start like this:

A: Aren't you . . . ?
B: Yes. We were in the same English class in . . . .
A: That's right. So what are you doing now?
B: Well, I . . . now. How about you? . . .

48

Language close-up

Watch the video and complete the conversation. Then practice it.

Marie Moore and Kate Davis have just arrived at their twentieth high school reunion.

Marie: Our class ...... *pictures* ...... !

Kate: Remember Ted Green? He was so ....

Marie: Yeah. And really .... , too. Remember .... out on the .... field?

Kate: How .... I forget? But I haven't .... him since .... What was he .... to do?

Marie: I think he .... to be an ....

Kate: That's .... He went .... to Los Angeles to .... school.

Marie: I would .... to see him again. I .... he comes ....

Kate: Me, too. I .... if he's ....

Marie: Yeah. Isn't this that .... from our .... class? What was his .... ?

Kate: Yeah, the .... one. Don .... He was easy to ....

Marie: Don Porter, ... was it. He .... ever said a ....

A Match phrases from A and B and write five sentences. Then compare with a partner.

A	B
Don Porter	decided to open a restaurant when she was going to culinary school.
Angela Lopez	was working on a novel when he met Angela Lopez.
Jenny Lindsay	has been working as a reporter for Channel 4.
Kate Davis	played football in high school and wanted to be an actor.
Ted Green	lost her job and has been looking for a new one for several weeks.

1. *Don Porter was working on a novel when he met Angela Lopez.*
2. ....
3. ....
4. ....
5. ....

B Now complete these sentences with information about yourself. Compare with a partner.

1. I was .... when I ....
2. While I was .... , I became interested in ....
3. I've been .... for the last ....

13 Street performers

1 CULTURE

Visitors exploring Seattle, Washington, should not miss the Pike Place Market. The market opened in 1907, when farmers began to sell their produce there. It is right by the water, and you can still buy fresh seafood. You can also buy cheese, spices, wines from the Northwest, tea, and coffee. What makes the Pike Place Market famous today, though, is the "free" entertainment. Every day the market fills with street performers and the people who come to watch them.

Are street performers popular in your country?
Would you stop to watch a street performer?
Do you think people should give money to street performers?
  Why or why not?

COME VISIT

FARMERS MARKET

open:
Mon. through Sat. 9:00 to 6:00
Sun. 11:00 to 5:00

the
PIKE PLACE MARKET
First Avenue at Pike Street

2 VOCABULARY Street performers

A *Pair work* Write the correct word(s) under each picture.

✓an acrobat   a juggler   a magician   a saxophone player   a string quartet   a vocal group

1. ....

2. *an acrobat* ....

3. ....

4. ....

5. ....

6. ....

B Can you think of four more types of street performers? Write them below.

1. .... 2. .... 3. .... 4. ....

3 GUESS THE FACTS

Watch the video with the sound off. What kinds of performers do you
see in the video? Circle them in Exercise 2.

Watch the video

4 GET THE PICTURE

Did people like the street
performers? Check (✓) the
correct answers. Then
compare with a partner.

liked by everyone	☐	☐	☐	☐
not really liked by some	☐	☐	☐	☐

5 WATCH FOR DETAILS

What are these people's opinions of the performers? Write at least one word.
Then compare with a partner.

	the saxophone player	*the magician*	*the string quartet*	*the juggler*
	entertaining			

WHAT'S YOUR OPINION?

A What did you think of the performers? Rate each performance from
1 (very good) to 5 (poor). Circle the numbers.

1. the saxophone player	2. the magician	3. the string quartet	4. the juggler	5. the vocal group
1	1	1	1	1
2	2	2	2	2
3	3	3	3	3
4	4	4	4	4
5	5	5	5	5

B *Pair work* Compare opinions. Choose words from the box or use
words of your own.

boring	funny	professional	silly
disappointing	nothing special	really good	unprofessional
entertaining	poor	relaxing	wonderful
fantastic			

A: What did you think of the saxophone player?
B: I thought he was really good. I gave him a 1. How about you? . . .

Follow-up

7 **HIRE A PERFORMER**

Group work Imagine you are planning a party and want to hire a performer
or group of performers. Which of these performers would you like to hire? Why?

A: I think it would be great to hire a magician.
B: Why?
A: Well, because magicians are entertaining. . . .

a clown	*a guitarist*	*a magician*	*a pianist*	*a rock band*

Language close-up

8 WHAT DID THEY SAY?

Watch the video and complete the interviews. Then compare with a partner.

Neil Murray is asking people what they thought of the saxophone player.

Neil: What did you ......*think*...... of the .... ?

Man 1: I .... it was very .... It was
.... It was ....
It was ....

Man 2: I was .... at how .... he was. I didn't
.... a person on the .... to just pick up
a .... and play that .... So I was
.... by that.

Woman 1: He was really .... It's .... to do that
by .... with no other background ....
or anything and make it .... really good. And he did
a good ....

9 PARTICIPLES Giving opinions

A Rewrite these sentences using present and past participles.
Then compare with a partner.

1. The vocal group entertained me.
   The vocal group was entertaining.
   I was entertained by the vocal group.

2. The juggler disappointed me.
   ....
   ....

3. The string quartet relaxed me.
   ....
   ....

4. The magician bored me.
   ....
   ....

B Now change your sentences to give your true opinions. Read them
to a partner.

C Complete the chart. Then compare with a partner.

Something you find entertaining	Something you find relaxing
I find .... *entertaining.*	....
Something you find disappointing	**Something you find boring**
....	....

Ms. Gardner's promotion

Preview

1 CULTURE

There have been many important changes in the United States in the last forty years. One of these is the number of working women. In 1960, only 37 percent of women worked, but in 1990, 57.5 percent worked outside the home. By the year 2005, that number may rise to 80 percent. However, not many women in the United States get promoted to management positions. Many experts think this is because women often have to leave their jobs when they have children. In 1995, 46 percent of the working people in the United States were women, but only 6.6 percent of managers and professionals – company executives, doctors, lawyers – were women.

Working People in the US, 1995

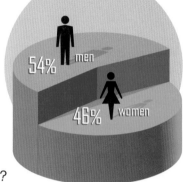

54% men
46% women

Do many women work in your country? Do women have jobs as managers? Do more women in your country work now than twenty or forty years ago? What kinds of jobs do they have?

2 VOCABULARY Emotions

Pair work What emotions do you think these people feel? Write one word under each picture.

annoyed   confused   embarrassed   nervous   pleased   ✓surprised

1. *surprised*

2. ....

3. ....

4. ....

5. ....

6. ....

3 GUESS THE STORY

Watch the first thirty seconds of the video with the sound off.
Do you think Julia Gardner's co-workers are happy about her promotion?
Why or why not?

Watch the video

4 GET THE PICTURE

Check (✓) the correct answers. Then compare with a partner.

1. Julia Gardner was promoted to ....
   ☐ marketing manager
   ☐ sales manager

2. Barbara is away from her desk
   because ....
   ☐ she has an appointment
   ☐ she's planning a party for Julia

5 WATCH FOR DETAILS

Put the pictures in order (1 to 6). Then write the correct sentence under each
picture. Compare with a partner.

Someone delivers flowers to the conference room.
✓ The company announces Julia's promotion.
Everyone congratulates Julia on her promotion.
At 1:30, Julia is still waiting for Barbara.

Julia wonders if people are upset
about her promotion.
Barbara tells Julia that she'll be
back by 1:00.

....
....

....
....

....
....

....
....

1

The company announces
Julia's promotion.

....
....

WHO SAID WHAT?

Who said the sentences below? Check (✓) the correct answers. Then compare with a partner.

	Julia	Barbara	Laurie
1. I wonder if people are upset.	☐	☐	☐
2. It probably means they're worried that things might change.	☐	☐	☐
3. Can you have lunch with me today?	☐	☐	☐
4. Maybe we can meet later this afternoon.	☐	☐	☐
5. Could you come into my office, please?	☐	☐	☐
6. I think she went to see the dentist.	☐	☐	☐
7. That's strange.	☐	☐	☐
8. The office staff isn't allowed to hold birthday parties.	☐	☐	☐
9. It's not what you think!	☐	☐	☐
10. You weren't supposed to come in yet!	☐	☐	☐

Follow-up

ROLE PLAY

Group work Work in groups of three and act out a conversation between Julia, Barbara, and Laurie. Use the sentences in Exercise 6 to help you. Start like this:

    Julia: Barbara, can I ask you something?
Barbara: Sure. . . .

GESTURES

Group work Play a game. Take turns acting out the following sentences from the video with appropriate gestures and/or facial expressions. Your classmates will try to guess which sentence you have chosen.

Gee, what a surprise!　　Oh? What do you mean?
What's going on?　　　　Wow! Look at that!
It's not what you think!　That's ridiculous.
How strange.　　　　　　Sorry about that.

Gee, what a surprise!

Language close-up

9 WHAT DID THEY SAY?

Watch the video and complete the conversation. Then practice it.

Julia Gardner's co-workers have just found out about her promotion.

Steve: Wow! Look at that. Julia ......*finally*........ got her
....

Ruth: Gee, what a .... !

Jerry: She must be .... about it. That probably
.... she'll .... to the head office.

Steve: Here she .... now. Time to .... back to work.

Julia: How .... ! . . . Barbara, . . .

Barbara: Yes?

Julia: Can I .... you something?

Barbara: ....

Julia: This .... sound crazy, but I wonder if people
are .... by my promotion.

Barbara: No, I'm .... everyone's .... for you.

Julia: It's just that . . . well, no one has .... anything to
.... , and sometimes I see people
....

Barbara: It .... means they're worried that things
.... change around here. You .... how
people .... change.

10 MODALS AND ADVERBS Expressing probability

A Complete each conversation with a logical answer. Then compare with a partner.

1. A: I just got a promotion, and I'm really happy. But sometimes I see people whispering.
   B: Maybe it means ....

2. A: My assistant wasn't free for lunch. And she looked a little uncomfortable.
   B: It could mean ....

3. A: My assistant had a meeting with me at 1:00, but it's 1:30 and she's still not back.
   B: It may mean ....

4. A: The staff isn't allowed to have parties, but someone just brought flowers into the conference room!
   B: Perhaps it means ....

B *Pair work* Now have similar conversations about
real or imaginary situations of your own.

A: My friend Steve is never free for lunch.
B: Maybe it means . . .

15 How embarrassing!

1 CULTURE

In a recent survey, people in the United States were asked to describe their most embarrassing moments during a visit to someone's home. Here are the top answers:

- Dressing wrong for the occasion.
- Arriving on the wrong day or at the wrong time.
- Spilling something or breaking something valuable.
- Saying something by mistake that offended the host.
- Forgetting someone's name.

Would the same things be embarrassing in your culture? Why or why not?

What was your most embarrassing moment during a visit to someone's home?

Almost everyone has dressed wrong at least once!

2 VOCABULARY Problems with guests

Pair work Do you know these nouns and verbs? Complete the chart. (If you don't know a word, look it up in your dictionary.) Then take turns answering the questions below.

Verb	Noun	Verb	Noun
apologize	....	misunderstand	....
....	approval	....	offer
invite	....	....	realization
....	lie	....	reminder

1. Have you apologized for anything recently?
2. What's a habit some people have that you don't approve of?
3. Who have you invited out recently?
4. What's something you might lie about?
5. Have you had a problem because someone misunderstood you recently?
6. Has someone offered you something nice recently?
7. What is something that you have realized about yourself?
8. Have you had to remind someone to do something lately?

③ GUESS THE FACTS

Watch the video with the sound off. What four embarrassing situations
do you see?

Watch the video

④ GET THE PICTURE

A What happened to these people? Write the numbers in the boxes.
Choose from the list below.

1. A dinner guest stayed too late at this person's house.
2. This person went to stay with a friend whose apartment was really dirty.
3. This person arrived too early for a party, and the hosts weren't ready.
4. A guest broke something valuable at this person's house.

B Now write at least one more piece of information on the lines.
Compare with a partner.

3

1 *host in old clothes*
   shower running

2 ....

3 ....

4 ....

C *Pair work* Take turns. Describe what happened to each person.

"This guy (*points to photo*) went to a party, but he arrived too early.
His hosts weren't ready. . . ."

How embarrassing! • 59

A What are these people's opinions about the situations? Write the correct number in each box. Then compare with a partner.

Situation 1
The guest should have . . .

The host should have . . .

1. apologized and offered to help.
2. pretended to have an errand to run.
3. left quickly and come back later.

1. asked the guest to help.
2. invited the guest in anyway.
3. asked the guest to come back later.

Situation 2
The host should have . . .

1. lied and said she had to get up very early.
2. pretended she wasn't tired.
3. reminded her boss that it was late.

Situation 3
The host should have . . .

1. said the lamp was old and wasn't important.
2. dropped a hint about the cost of antiques.
3. told her friend to buy a new lamp.

Situation 4
The guest should have . . .

1. just accepted the situation.
2. offered to help clean up.
3. gone to a hotel.

B *Pair work* Which people do you agree with? Take turns sharing your opinions.

A: I agree with her (*points to photo*). The guest should have . . .
B: I think his suggestion is better (*points*). The guest should have . . .

Follow-up

6 *WHAT WOULD YOU HAVE DONE?*

Group work Take turns describing awkward or embarrassing situations you've been in. Say what you did. Your classmates will tell you what they would have done.

A: I realized I forgot my best friend's birthday, so I gave her some flowers two weeks later and apologized. What would you have done?
B: Well, I think I would have . . .

Language close-up

7 *WHAT DID THEY SAY?*

People are describing embarrassing things that happened to them.

A Watch the first situation. Complete the guest's description.

I was ....*invited*........ to a .... , and I arrived a .... hour
.... I thought it would .... me .... to get
.... Well, the .... came to the door .... old
clothes and holding a .... cleaner. I could .... a shower
.... in the background, and on .... of that, not a
.... guest was ....

B Now watch the second situation. Complete the host's description.

I .... my boss to .... the other ....
She was .... a great .... and wouldn't ....
By .... , my .... and I were so
.... Finally, my husband fell .... at the
.... My boss was very .... when she
.... it was so ....

8 WOULD HAVE *AND* SHOULD HAVE *Giving suggestions*

Pair work Can you think of suggestions for these situations? Write statements using **would have** and **should have**. Then compare around the class. Who has the best suggestions?

1. A guest arrived on the wrong day for the party.
   The guest *should have apologized and gone home* .
   If I were the host, I *would have* ....

2. A dinner guest broke a valuable dish.
   If I were the guest, I ....
   The host ....

3. Two dinner guests got into a big argument.
   The guests ....
   If I were the host, I ....

4. The host discovered she didn't have enough food.
   The guests ....
   If I were the host, I ....

A wonderful evening

Preview

 ### 1 *CULTURE*

Young adults in the United States and Canada often invite the person they're dating to their home for dinner. It's a chance to meet the parents and mix with the family. If you're invited to a friend's house, ask if there's anything you can bring. Then arrive on time with a small gift. Before dinner, ask if you can help with the preparations. During the meal, make small talk as you eat. If you enjoy the food, it's polite to ask for a second helping. After dinner, ask if you can help with the dishes. Plan to stay for a while to play games or talk with your friend's family.

Do young people in your country invite their boyfriends or girlfriends home for dinner?

What rules should dinner guests follow in your culture?

Young people also do things outside the home on dates, like go to the movies.

2 *VOCABULARY* Adjectives

Pair work How would you feel in the situations below? Choose adjectives from the box.

amused	delighted	enthusiastic	nervous	shy
angry	disappointed	excited	pleased	upset
bored	embarrassed	interested	relaxed	worried

1. You are going to meet your girlfriend or boyfriend's parents.

   A: I think I'd feel nervous.
   B: Really? I'd be excited.

2. You are a dinner guest at someone's house. Your host offers you food you don't like.
3. Your best friend gives you a gift that you really like.
4. Someone forgets an appointment with you.
5. You meet someone you like at a party. The next day you run into the person at the supermarket.
6. You are going on a date with someone you don't know well. Your new friend is wearing clothes that you think look strange.

Watch the first minute of the video with the sound off.
Where do you think Bob is going? Check (✓) your answer.

Bob

☐ to a wedding
☐ to meet his girlfriend's parents
☐ to a movie with his girlfriend

Watch the video

4 GET THE PICTURE

How do you think these people really felt? Look carefully at their
facial expressions in the video and check (✓) the best answers.
Then compare with a partner.

1. How did Bob feel before he left home?
   ☐ relaxed   ☐ nervous

2. Did Helen like the perfume that Bob gave her?
   ☐ definitely   ☐ probably not

3. How does Helen's father feel about acting?
   ☐ a little unenthusiastic   ☐ very unenthusiastic

4. Did Bob enjoy the fish stew?
   ☐ definitely   ☐ not really

5. Did Bob want to play Scrabble after dinner?
   ☐ yes   ☐ no

5 MAKING INFERENCES

Who said what? Check (✓) the person who said each sentence. Did the people really mean what they said? Did they just want to be polite? On the lines, write **S** for sincere or **P** for polite. Compare with a partner.

	Man	Woman	Older man
1. You know I don't like Scrabble.	✓ _S_	☐	☐
2. This is one of my favorite perfumes.	☐	☐	☐
3. I'm really interested in the theater.	☐	☐	☐
4. I think I may try to get into law school.	☐	☐	☐
5. He's such a sweetie, isn't he?	☐	☐	☐
6. It's one of my favorite dishes.	☐	☐	☐
7. I knew this was going to be a wonderful evening.	☐	☐	☐

Follow-up

6 POLITE RESPONSES

A *Pair work* Imagine you're at a friend's house for dinner. Complete the conversations below with polite responses. Then act them out.

1. A: Why don't we play chess? It's one of my favorite games!
   B: *It's one of my favorite games, too.*

2. A: My brother is a great guy, isn't he?
   B: ....

3. A: We're having something special for dinner. I hope you like spicy food!
   B: ....

4. A: I bought this painting at an art show. I hope you like it!
   B: ....

B Now act out at least two new conversations of your own. You can make them long or short. Make sure not to hurt your partner's feelings!

7 WHAT DID THEY SAY?

Watch the video and complete the conversation. Then practice it.

Bob is getting ready to meet his girlfriend's parents for the first time.

Bob: Well, ...*how*... do I .... ?
Mother: Fine, just .... You look very ....
Bob: Are you .... ? Is this .... OK?
Mother: You look .... There's no .... to be
....
Bob: But I'm .... Helen's .... for
the first ....
Mother: Don't .... I'm sure they're .... nice.
.... will be OK.
Josh: How about a .... of .... before you
.... ? It will help you ....
Bob: Thanks, Josh, but you .... I don't .... Scrabble.
.... , I really have to ....

8 REPORTED SPEECH Giving opinions

A Report what Bob and Helen said. Then compare with a partner.

1. "I don't like Scrabble." (Bob)
   Bob said he didn't like Scrabble.

2. "I'm meeting Helen's parents for the first time." (Bob)

3. "I don't like fish stew." (Bob)

4. "This is one of my favorite perfumes." (Helen)

5. "I'm really interested in the theater." (Bob)

6. "I may try to get into law school." (Bob)

You know I don't like fish stew.

B *Class activity* Ask several classmates what they think of the things in the box. Write down their answers. Then report their opinions to the class.

A: What do you think of boxing?
B: I think it's awful.
A: Tina said she thought boxing was awful. . . .

boxing
card games
cigarette smoke
rap music
spicy food
strong perfume
tennis

Acknowledgments

Author's Acknowledgments

A great number of people assisted in the development of the Video Program. Particular thanks go to the following:

The **students** and **teachers** in the following schools and institutes who pilot-tested the Videos or the Video Activity Books; their valuable comments and suggestions helped shape the content of the entire program:

Athenée Français, Tokyo, Japan; **Centro Cultural Brasil-Estados Unidos**, Belém, Brazil; **Eurocentres**, Virginia, U.S.A.; **Fairmont State College**, West Virginia, U.S.A.; **Hakodate Daigaku**, Hokkaido, Japan; **Hirosaki Gakuin Daigaku**, Aomori, Japan; **Hiroshima Shudo Daigaku**, Hiroshima, Japan; **Hokkaido Daigaku, Institute of Language and Cultural Studies**, Hokkaido, Japan; **The Institute Meguro**, Tokyo, Japan; **Instituto Brasil-Estados Unidos**, Rio de Janeiro, Brazil; **Instituto Cultural de Idiomas**, Caxias do Sul, Brazil; **Instituto Cultural Peruano-Norteamericano**, Lima, Peru; **Musashino Joshi Daigaku**, Tokyo, Japan; **Nagasaki Gaigo Tanki Daigaku**, Nagasaki, Japan; **New Cida**, Tokyo, Japan; **Parco-ILC English School**, Chiba, Japan; **Pegasus Language Services**, Tokyo, Japan; **Poole Gakuin Tanki Daigaku**, Hyogo, Japan; **Seinan Gakuin Daigaku**, Fukuoka, Japan; **Shukugawa Joshi Tanki Daigaku**, Hyogo, Japan; **Tokai Daigaku**, Kanagawa, Japan; **YMCA Business School**, Kanagawa, Japan; and **Yokohama YMCA**, Kanagawa, Japan.

The **editorial** and **production** team:
Sylvia P. Bloch, David Bohlke, Karen Brock, Jeff Chen, Karen Davy, Yuri Hara, Pam Harris, Paul Heacock, Louisa Hellegers, Pauline Ireland, Lise R. Minovitz, Pat Nelson, Kathy Niemczyk, Danielle Power, Carrie Ryan, Mary Sandre, Tami Savir, Karen Sullivan, Kayo Taguchi, Louisa van Houten, Mary Vaughn, Jennifer Wilkin, and Dorothy Zemach.

And Cambridge University Press **staff** and **advisors**:
Jim Anderson, Angela Andrade, Mary Louise Baez, Carlos Barbisan, Kathleen Corley, Kate Cory-Wright, Elizabeth Fuzikava, Steve Golden, Cecilia Gomez, Heather Gray, Bob Hands, Ken Kingery, Gareth Knight, Nigel McQuitty, João Madureira, Andy Martin, Alejandro Martinez, Carine Mitchell, Mark O'Neil, Tom Price, Dan Schulte, Catherine Shih, Howard Siegelman, Ivan Sorrentino, Alcione Tavares, Koen Van Landeghem, and Ellen Zlotnick.

And a special thanks to the video producer, Master Communications Group.

Illustrators

Adventure House 6, 10 (*top*), 16 (*bottom*), 17, 18 (*top*), 42, 44, 50 (*top*)
Keith Bendis 12, 22 (*top*), 25, 26, 38 (*top*), 46, 52, 58, 62 (*bottom*)
Daisy de Puthod 14 (*bottom*), 18 (*bottom*), 29, 30 (*bottom*), 35

Wally Neibart 10 (*bottom*), 16 (*top*), 20 (*bottom*), 24, 34 (*top*), 38 (*middle*), 40, 48, 50 (*bottom*), 57, 62 (*top*)
Andrew Toos 4, 14 (*top*), 22 (*bottom*), 30 (*top*), 34 (*bottom*), 41, 45, 49, 64

Photo credits

Photo researcher: Sylvia P. Bloch
2 © Don Klumpp/The Image Bank
6 © Al Harvey/T.W.'s Image Network
8 (*Stanley Park*) © Images B.C./T.W.'s Image Network; (*seaplane*) © Al Harvey/T.W.'s Image Network; (*Chinatown*) © Gunter Marx/T.W.'s Image Network
20 (*from left*) © Explorer/Photo Researchers; © Blair Seitz/Photo Researchers; © John Kelly/The Image Bank

26 Hot Diggety Dogger courtesy of Concepts Electronix, Inc.
44 (*handicrafts*) Chris Corrie © used by permission of the Santa Fe Convention & Visitors Bureau; (*southwestern food*) © Obremski/The Image Bank; (*San Miguel Mission*) © Joanna McCarthy/The Image Bank

All other photographs by Rick Armstrong and John Hruska